Birds I Cannot Name

Birds I Cannot Name

Poems

Damien Uriah

Fort Smith, Arkansas

Birds I Cannot Name

Cover image: *Young girl with flowers in front of a window* (ca. 1936-1942), Maurice Denis

Author photo: Allyson Lovell

Edited by Casie Dodd
Design & typography by Belle Point Press

Belle Point Press, LLC
Fort Smith, Arkansas
bellepointpress.com
editor@bellepointpress.com

Find Belle Point Press
on Facebook, Substack,
and Instagram (@bellepointpress)

Printed in the United States of America

29 28 27 26 25 1 2 3 4 5

Library of Congress Control Number: 2025934499

ISBN: 978-1-960215-35-2

BICN/BPP45

Contents

Two

One

Migrating Psalm

1.

Funny,
the dead have never been this close—
why nothing speaks.

For another I dreamed of old buildings
in Stilwell. The walls billowed like hung blankets.
Something was handed to me.

And for my friend the musician
I took up Buddhism.
He left a desire to follow a marked path.

Before, even when awake, I saw the apparitions.
A white tail crossed the road in front of the pick-up truck
which carried the midwife who first held each of my siblings.

Riding along, my foot behind the head of the casket,
I made sure she did not slide off onto the road
and swore it was her pale spirit leaping the barbed wire.

2.

I was on the bus. February had become the worst month.
Snow drift—a fence half buried as if in cold salt.

The plateau wind through the broadside
window

entered my body.

I thought it was you.
I thought you had gone from your suffering at last.

But it would be days.

3.

I want you to know

I returned to the side of the mountain.   I saw the string of hills carry your
rivers of fog

and believed (after Sarah told me)   that day you made the weather.

But what I noticed without any help

was a screaming hawk in the trees. I put a dull piece of sandstone in my pocket,

though somewhere I have discarded the stone you painted gold.

I am sorry I could not tell you before.

4.

Can people (when they die I mean) inhabit the bodies of animals?
That would be wonderful.

With the living I have fallen
into hoping this is true.

If it is, will you come find me
though I have gone west again?

Meet me in the coyote or moose?
Sometimes there are ravens. You'd like their cleverness.

I know. I know we're not familiar
with the paths through these seasons

but when spring brings back the sound in trees
I will be sure to say something

though I don't think I remember
how to pray.

Scattered Leaves

Ripe blackberries by
the path. Wet, sticky fingers.
One more failed errand.

Pokeberries grow in
graywater. A purple hand
printed on his chest.

The old mothers still cry
and the winds bend the oak trees
like they used to.

Man in Cedar Rocking Chair

Steady inhalation
          through the windows
of a stone house.

The box fan pirouettes outer heavens
          into the heavens of the knees.

Occasional voices
and behind them a shard note   thin

and not really anywhere
residual in the old sawyer's ears.

Eyes shut
his sight   sails over dark water.

In Vietnam he still carries a canteen.
Yellow starred flags float on the stream.

As painted clouds
          blue and red billowing fabrics

slip away, wet corners arched in
toward heaven.

And heaven is different in his reasoning
          depending on the season.

The sap of late autumn
          is black on his hands.

(At the Community) She Used to Walk So Often in Darkness

Before tar and gravel,
yellow sneezeweed dotted early night
on the rise in the middle of the road
returning to path with growth.
Progress was another word, another place.

A child without shoes heard stutters in long grass
having faith without cause
while pond frogs mourned the summer.
Cool air settling in the dust, the gathering season had come.

She could not know the history of that place her parents chose
or the earth memory embedding in her naked toes,
or the source of collective heart which had opened the doors of the houses
when it was time for heading to high pasture
to tabernacle under sky's winged horse.

She could not know the trance of false day in cities, or better
or worse, the venom of her sylvan separation,
the minds seers and scarcities make
of good believers.

She did know darkness
reveals a better light
in logs lifted by fire—a starry night
and the solitude of a whole shadowed village,
knew her fathers' guitars and the lyrics of laughter
and her mothers' orders over supper.
There was still time.

Evening Leads a Boy along Rivers

Wild gathered cedar and pine free birds you cannot name
into late light, welcoming each of them as moments
into her darkening sea, her wholeness falling on footprints.

Listen, she says, these graves are speaking.

Epithets you have offered here and now float awhile
like logs in this confluence of the Poteau and the Arkansas,
but the forgotten who are still here have also named these rivers.

Stained wings lift like waves.
The white egret captures pieces of her sky.

Her gift is to strike until you fall backward onto the anthill.

They crawl into your clothes
to say what are you
and welcome.

What She Said When I First Came to the Community

In this place the bare trees of winter learn to sing.
In this place is the psalm of god.

I was born in the light of spring,
in the rain, and from that moment on
I have been evaporating.

In this place are warring tongues
and men with guns, our people
who lost themselves to belief,

but the fields continue to give grass
and the goats still jump the fence
and we learn our bodies in the old bus by the gully,

dust from the chicken coop in our lungs.
Don't choke on chicken shit.
Cover your mouth or lose something.

Remember to go every once in a while
a little further down the gully where
the water escapes and never stops running
deeper and deeper into the valley of god.

And what if we were naked,
two children alone in a creek-bed,
and we were far from this place
so I asked you what it was you thought you were
and I kept asking until you had no answer

and we kept praying, kept slipping away
as streams over red clay and sandstone.
Deeper and deeper into the Ozarks
where the water changes direction.

On Falling onto a Dead Woman as a Young Boy

It is difficult to remember.
I didn't touch her but caught myself
on the seams
of white burial gown

then my vision went
to April two years before
when everyone shared white ice cream
and fruit flies with fruit.

In celebration of her husband
  the gardener
  now a garden,
  I watched a white head of clover
  mark the end of winter.

After he died I never saw her
until she testified in meeting two years later—
two days before those boys
would call it a secret
and lead me to the back room to push me in.

This poem is supposed to be about falling
into that coffin, but when I think about it
I always end up somewhere else—
near the last time I heard her voice.

She sings beautifully that Sunday morning. I will always remember
as if by natural selection her face when she was alive

and the shafts of spring's sun in the meetinghouse
and nothing said.

The clear sky of her face.
She has forgotten something I am just learning
though I don't know what, or how
a face can look like the sky, but it does.

Ozark Psalm

The opened west window of a single-wide
saturates with the hand-turn of the lightbulb
as the woman of the last house
begins to prepare a lonely supper.
In time this wet breeze fills with the balm
of her wild herbs baked in unleavened bread
and goat meat fried in butter. Yes lord,
she hears the woods, the sheep's bleat beyond those coyotes
and the closer quaver of a shore willow's lichened arms.
What was below the surface of her pond rises in darkness
turning her ears toward a steady wild of voices
she has always known. Here,
bullfrogs and cicadas do not call without meaning
so she scribbles on a page on the counter
while an insect inspects the smell of that ink
and glossolalia bleeds on the back of her mouth,
trembling . . .
Birds she cannot name
fly over in the dark . . . fickle . . . mona ha a ha.
From the throat she declares
their black praises in the key of spring.

Practicing Sadness

Samuel lay in clovers, having followed a sense of falling there—
that curious desire he sometimes got when riding a bicycle
to let gravity lead, to release the handlebars
and lift hands and eyes, to lean left then right.

He collapsed with an invisible forgiving
and satisfying force beside the sidewalk.
There he would work to perfect his art

with awkward enunciations of the new melody.
Like a pencil pushed to page with too much pressure
or the bold lines of an odd circle and no light use of erasure.

Arms out, head tilted just melancholic the child concentrated
on longing after pale stars in the dome of firmament
and softly said to passersby heading in for evening meeting
that he was just fine.

Mush

In this place you have the mind and body of a boy,
heavy with the oils of mountain and first kiss: your responsibilities.
But you pretend more weight in the thought of leaving school.

Your mother won't let you drop out for "what work for whose money?"
though there is nothing for breakfast but corn-meal mush and sugar
which has thickened into the worst enemy of her family's mornings.

Your younger brother is refusing to finish his mush
so he will eat it for lunch, and he will not have mashed potatoes
and that is that. To prove his sincerity, he runs to the toilet and vomits.

In this place it is not your brother's misery over corn-meal mush
making you desire what has already come. Work means eating
frosted corn flakes for breakfast, like your father at his new house.

For now you must go to school. You lift and push open the screen door,
the hinges rusted halfway gone. Daddy used pine scraps. They are rotting.

Each a Member

Just now mallards lifting from a still pool
sound like wheels breaking free from axles,
their feathers forcing air to recognize
the mallard self.
Each member offers their body to the falling sun,
and shadows wander out from their edges
plaquing the land with definition.

The air shifts slightly like the light,
and dark opposites appear.
Gathered quail and lines of mice
scatter among their others.

Each life here translates into river,
willows bending along the wind
and big stones like altars against current,
a curve and thrust of water
whose stream will walk into a closer state of present
who sits down behind the world.

Labor in Spring

The young leaves are filling the gaps in the forest
So that this earth seems smaller but with more edges.
I dig swales next to new fruit trees as the storm clouds
Tease rain. She prays they leave a little water this time.
It has been a dry spring. We have had to hang our worry
Over the fence like a rug. Maybe the summer coming
Will be wetter than usual. Maybe fields won't dry
Before September. Maybe the child following
Sunbeams to the next world will really have just been a dream,
And the young mother's crying will bring a downpour.
If only the rain would dare to bring him back.
Eat wild onion bread while it's hot, Uncle, Auntie, says our boy from whom
We have hidden the recent disappearance of a new friend.
The warm light falls out of clouds. We are empty at noontime.

He Knew No Haste

Because we could not stop for death
A rusted van follows a road on the forest hill
My child belted to the back seat
Witnessing the passing world from a window
Wide eyes running away with red trees
Reaching for the vaulted sky
Where the labor of night ends
In the first freedom of a red heart
Who wants to be the sunrise
Heading west as far as west goes
No one who knows him going ahead
Knowing that we are all
A valley of lights returning
All eyes of invisible all
The wind moving as the pines
All returning with all
Between the rain drops
Where we can't see
Only the hush of the lake in the valley
The quiet gospel of a beaver
Bronze light on wet fur on the work bent back
Only the hallways of a house on the hill
And waiting for our voices
And the old walls to come back
Together
Who will speak to us in the night
There are only ghosts
Sleeping in the shadows
Where the crowded oaks are

Carved by invisible teeth
Sharpening spears on the shore
Taking him
Where nothing makes
A sound where there is

Samuel

(From the Covenant Man, Who Weather-Proofed Wood with Used Motor Oil and Diesel)

He was always shoveling without shoes so I said his toes were soft as yellow potatoes; the ones the shovel splits in half when you're digging them up. Half of him was rooted to the harvest, but half was left out rotting in the sun. I didn't know what would happen to him, or I wouldn't have cut-up about splittin' flesh.

Him and his grandma were maple copters spun from the same tree. She married for God, before marrying for love, before marrying again to get away. Samuel never met her, but his face followed in her sunlight. We're tethered to movement, she told me once. When everyone was still alive I knew we'd make a history; but everything turned to yellow blades of sunflower or went up with the fire in '72.

> Have you seen Mary? She's supposed to help me with this cell phone. I don't get *all* that monthly check, and I got to call your Papa. The Lord has a word for him. He's trying to pastor God's sheep when there're only wolves and covenants burning like goat hide.

Pretending to hold up the sky with his hands, he always said "summer makes blades of yellow sunflowers" and never wore shoes and got tangled in stories like purple snap peas get tangled in fence. He saw faces in those flowers and like them was born and gone before age. He liked the feel of saying he slept in a cottonmouth's mouth.

> Have you seen her? She's supposed to help me with this phone. I need to talk to your Papa 'cause God's working in me today. They must be visions,'cause they haven't pulled the trigger. I swear, it's like there're men with guns behind them rocks.

Samuel's hair was like yellow blades of sunflower the day he died. I was teaching him to work iron, but he was leaving again before long. I told him how half worthless he was right before the welds gave out and I rode an I-beam thirty feet to the ground, managing to keep about half my bones from breaking. Samuel held up the sky with his fast hands as a piece of sheet iron took him away.

Driving to Work

Apparitions which gathered through my sleep
crumble like old buildings in this sun-born mist.
Driving the dead asphalt through half-eyed chills
I blink a half-daze while the white moon splits.
My specters carry into the brightening day.

The bird who sang behind my sleep now orders silence.
Lowering the window, I inhale the real, damp air
so we can crawl together over this bluing landscape
until every soil tooth sinks into our raw skins.
Mother earth's wild haunting to fulfill us.

My van is rusting and the suspension is shotty
but I've no bootstraps, just this van to pull me up
against my heartbeat's will to go gently. I tire these last miles
running to and from rich men's land. No place man. Smoke and sand.

Two Instances of Samuel's Unknowing

At a kitchen counter with coffee and blueprints, the old man he works for asks him to guess at all the salvageable elements of the fallen barn out back. Samuel must have some idea since it was he who suggested taking material from that old feature in order to construct the new shed. He must sit with the man. He must watch him use pen and paper. He must tell the man how many two-bys—how many four-bys he thinks are still good. Does he imagine the plywood will have lasted these rainy years? The man was successful in life, an engineer, and he's always kind enough to show Samuel, on paper, all the things Samuel fails to foresee. And Samuel must admit it is true. He has no fucking idea. He explains that he will only know what is still good after he has offered his body to the fallen barn.

•

Samuel dreams in lawn-mower lines. He lives in a yellow, vinyl complex. The best part of him sits on a patch of uncut grass surrounded on all sides by asphalt in early sun, early in the year. Yellow dandelions provide small relief to a starving bee. He takes witness for a moment and returns to reading a story about a burning-barrel and missing home so bad he can smell it. It is true, plastic seems to disappear when burned. But that is the kind of prayer that does not work anymore. There is the well-worn tradition of giving problems to the air. But that is no longer enough.

Rain on that Almost-Husband of Hers

I bore the hot wind blowing into his papa's truck
while he held his head out the window
searching the ditch for laying stones.
His mamma lived in the rock house his daddy built before he left
and the outer wall beneath the kitchen window needed fixing.

Back then I was young, childless. I just wanted to ride.
My gaze drifted from the window
as I listened to the static of tires on gravel. He stopped
and stepped out. I just thought he'd found a good rock
until I looked up and he's standing
near the carcass of a large animal hanging from the fence.

I couldn't count the times he cussed that millionaire
for surrounding a thousand good acres with 12-foot fence.
They'd made a killing charging people
to shoot the fat, corn-fed game trapped inside.

I was just learning how good that land had been—
that creek, those gullies and overhangs
"taught everyone he knew everything they knew"
before the Texas rancher put the land to use.

He had said the fences cut straight through deer trails
and that he'd seen them running
confused; that passing cars would spook them
into attempting the leap.

I didn't imagine I'd see it: the young buck's
antlers caught, body all contorted, maggots in the eyes,
face and mouth mangled.

But despite all that previous moaning
right then Samuel couldn't cuss. He wouldn't say nothing
about that rancher. He just stared into the field
like a sick fawn counting breaths.

the Water is in me

Vessel of Water. Pourer of Water
Laughter
louder than i can speak
like the drone of Pianos
like piano Clouds full of Rain
ready to burst from me

the Smile in your Stockings
dances in our Room and i leak
Water my Cries in the Corner
i am finally saved

holy Piano holy Stocking holy
Waves over my Arteries
holy Iceland
We will go together just you and
i love just You and i
trade the Spells for the Tundra
endlessly spill

holy open Sea   holy sing to me   holy i am free   holy Anything

i scream and you disappear. i am
Water the Water is in me. i am Rain,
and you are Clay
the Piano stops and i pool

Rain on that Almost-Husband of Hers

I told mamma   Samuel could convince a prisoner
to appreciate their solitude   that wasn't it.

I didn't think him a salesman.

I really meant his grit was contagious,
that I believed him when he said I was more than my job.

Because he was clueless,
because he was too honest,
and didn't own nothing,
because he'd given up thinking he was poor.
What I needed then.

Snow Falls from Branches

Should have found a job by now; should have slept in the night;
should have boiled old coffee before noon.
Instead, I wince at mid-day half-light. Through the only window,
it reinvents this small apartment I will lose at the end of January.

I will choose to notice this unhurried moment, so I can bring it back
into the sweet salvation of the dream of winter,
the dream in which I am drying and sorting husks from seed.

Outside, the occasioned wind makes a dusting of snow leap
from ponderosa needles into the air, carrying daylight to the earth.
And thicker, blind white clusters lapse from bare aspen.
I think of how this is like a secondary snowfall
but with an even softer rhythm—like an accent on emptiness.

Beyond the trees however, cars groan over a highway.
I can hear them through the walls
running to a call to which perhaps, for survival, I should respond.

But then I remember a sermon I heard as a child.
The good Lord's work
is already finished.

Rain on that Almost-Husband of Hers

You might think
he was of that rotten sort

with wandering minds   despite the spit in their hearts

who end up driving their fists
through our good walls at best.

Samuel was the son of a firewood hauler
and had no choice but to burn the last miles of an old van

driving into town   to become a demolition man

a roofer, sider,
mower of the ornate and unfruitful.

And I'm older now. I get it.
It was better to give up early.

Even if it was his last forty bucks   the relief of a cold 30

and gas to take him as far as the creek
is always better than a clear mind on a workday.

And gazing at growing old
breathing concrete dust and asbestos

and the dumbass foremen   always on power trips

and the fucking architects
with their hard-hats they don't need

and pouring concrete over good growing ground.

Debt

Red and golden illuminated
cars barrel through fog and rain.

They scream behind the world,

an interstate of sterilized
hurt under construction

augmenting the fields.

I Have Come into a Place Where There Is No Light

"Watchman remember," says the old woman
sowing sunflower seeds in the courtyard of my body
calling to that frightened presence in the tower,
"Tell me of the night, if it promise bear."

The watchman replies,
Great Mother! The moon is hidden
and has been taken from us for some time.

"Watchman remember that river to Orion
and the boat we built for sailing there
from the pasture break on a forest hill.
Watchman recall the old tower burning
in the breath of our boy's first freedom.
The light it made.

But still the darkness of a tent in the forest
on an island, those small hours,
eyes spilling into the dark,
the lizard enclosed with us reminding us
we could never be alone, no matter the distance.

Together we discovered
that it was not a sky god in his grandfather
who gathered the people on the east-facing slope
but Big Round Mountain which reaped
the scattered for its own sake.

The seed of disenfranchised
we were thrown into the center of a cosmos.
We were born in the arms of that mountain.
What payment for praise!

Now tell me of the night. Does it bear our beloved?"

The watchman weeps:
Those buildings, crawling over the land,
that is my fault! I am responsible for this insatiable hunger.

"Watchman remember that green hollow near the HUD-houses
where the putrid waters gather sediment
and rare species of eager grass.
The amphibians chose that place to test their songs
and there migrating birds find oasis.

Trust there comes a bright, contagious light on the horizon.
Following fires, our boy took the jug of wine
that was offered by a stranger's hands.

Look again to the night."

Rain on that Almost-Husband of Hers

I could have found someone afraid to be idle

a pink collar always measuring itself

                    but pesky ancestral spirits   kept telling me

though he was acting like a child   and though he was drunk

they had tasted something worth saving   in his bone marrow.

Most die unable to change.   Samuel was fluid and sour-sweet

lemonade spit   in the same face
that had made our lives inhuman.

The Dirt Road as Threshold

I drive the ranch ridge at noon
windows rolled down, dashboard rattling.
Pine saplings lie limp
in the heat. My memory
is an aging dog sitting shotgun,
scanning the red ditch
through mineral-clouded well-water eyes.

These hills have lost more woods.
The sky grown again, a young buck hangs
dead in high fence by the road.
So much is my fault.

Before I ran I was gifted apple trees,
and when I cleared
the tall hickory from the hillside
they called it "claiming."

I nearly thanked grandpa's god
when my mother called to tell me
those young trees choked in wild
blackberries because I left.

Though the city's been weaning me from sense
of activity in absence
these hills still complain like old women.
They start raising Cain as soon as I ease
the truck to a stop and kill the engine.

The dog leaps out of the window
to chase a roadrunner he will not catch
while the new black cows mock the heron.

In the side-mirror I swear
I see the ghost face of that preacher.
He keeps his hand on the plow I could not hold
as it rusts in the field.

Rain on that Almost-Husband of Hers

About the time I got pregnant, he quit a good job
to help an old man pick apples threatening to break the branches of trees.
I was sure the man barely paid Samuel enough for gas to get out of town,
but he was more than happy to quit the city for a week.

He stayed in their house. The man and his wife fed him three meals a day while he was picking.
I got a text from Samuel in the middle of the week
saying he'd take me out to a fancy restaurant when he got back.
By Thursday evening I got another message saying, "Well, maybe I'll just bring supper."

When he arrived at my mamma's house I saw him jump out the bed of a pickup truck.
He beat his hand on the tailgate and cussed like a happy drunk
with a driver I'd never met.
When he came to the door he was smiling. His van had broken down
so he'd left it back at the orchard. He had a full paper sack in his hands.

After giving me a big kiss on the face, he seemed pleased with himself and said,
"I have run out of money. But I brought apples."

Without a Useful Language I Must Warn the Birds

I have walked past the morning's last geese
with nothing really, skipping stones for prayers.
I search briars and branches covering roots
and survey wasted grass for gifts.

The sort of worldly light that does not compete with stars
falls from a sweetgum.
It is late November. Spiked orbs have begun claiming their tracts of earth.
They contain seeds fated to fight in the spring
for their stolen endowment.

This shade is imperfect, speckling.

North-born birds rise from the field and follow
each dutiful other over this tree and the Arkansas River.
They leave this grass as though it will last forever.

Note to Reader:

This book is a plastic bucket with air holes.

Yes, this bucket contains a few lives, like crawdads, little possibilities of time.

I have rarely existed outside of this bucket. We don't exist in most of times.
I am absent from some, yet in others only you are absent.

But in one time I know you
as a wild-haired child in a garden bursting with sunflowers.

In another you have never seen a sunflower in real life.

In yet another time I find you bleeding out
having lost a foot's worth of toes under a steel shovel.

In yet another time we are blue birds.

Gone North in a Crooked Line

Miles from our toes together in red mud
I remove my shoes and think myself strange
walking in crystal clear water, watching
the sun-fall and our decade
die with the light going back to you.

Birds rise from the river
in the only way the river knows.

Moments gathered when I was out of work, in a small city which, according to a woman from Seattle, had not found its identity.

It is early spring.

A marsh blackbird on a cattail's haggard stock knows I am watching

and displays the bright color

within his midnight wing.

Hardened snow in hemlock shade

while a legion of bulbs emerge

out of thawing earth.

I is many.

Starlings murmurate

above an abandoned grain silo.

Below the muted rainbow of top feathers the underbellies burst,

mirroring broad clouds drifting south.

Red-beaked mergansers do their diving

Beneath seeded maples bent over the river.

A thousand little pairs of wings.

With a length of willow cut by a beaver

a small girl makes figure eight

in the gray surface of cold sand.

A swallow clears remnants of past seasons

from her hole in the packed orange earth of Latah's bank

which borders our field of human dead.

At the Confluence of Latah Creek and the Spokane

the present word sleeps
in a wet tennis shoe laid on a tarp
while the nameless bird sings from the south
as if resting in the sky
in another world the river woman sneaks up behind me
her footprints travelling as rocks

the green hands of trees
needles, ovals, nameless shapes
capturers of wind
the winds recognition

the gray hands of the far roads
snake lines dug in the mountain
capturers of persons

the brown hands of the mountain
are rounded, worn fingers
capturers of cloud
the sky's recognition

the green hands grow on the brown hands
do they know of the brown hands as they drink
from their bodies

the white hands of the clouds
grow sick, amorphous, whimsical
capturers of the burning
supplicants of the perfect soul

the water will awaken this dead the water
will awaken this dead one day but for now

the people of the sun are waiting

The Fall in the City

Outside the branches of this willow

microplastic spins with rain-water
off studded tires. A plane cries across a cauldron of sky.
From concrete cubes on the sixth story, compressors clank and bawl,
hauling air through hoses. Blasts shriek steel in granite.

I pray for this perennial soul's overflow

to be a crown of plain, slow breaths falling quietly through noise
to become not much of a barrier but a circle nonetheless
made of what leaves are made.
Little blades of sun sinking toward a center
are no defense at all
but they are my only and cherished defense.

I have already seen the way

the mowing machines will take
these little pieces of light from me—
the ones I gathered on this page. Only black
branches which avoid ground will remain.
We will have failed our children who are still soil.
The nutrients of summer will be gathered up and bagged.

So now I write only to say I saw

the little sun spirits before they were taken.
They are shaped like light spread with a knife
on water. I wish a photograph could matter.
I would take these with me to wherever or heaven.
But it seems we must run now. Do we run toward heaven
to forget the sun and the ways it is given?

Spring in the City

People rev their engines, and she becomes afraid
and wishes to be in this moment differently.
She wants to be a water-bird carried on the rapids
knowing that anywhere, downriver, she might find food.
She just might find a table set by her grandmother,
and strawberries blended with cold milk.

But that is not why she is here.
She has come to this place to gather gray gravel in her hands
and to lather it into her face so that it bleeds. To become someone else.
The bush buds grow. The chipmunk emerges.
The weasel can have the visage of a bear.
She *is* capable of living in the city. These are not walls
though the mind would have them be; though the mind
has not caught up with its own experience.
Rain feels as if her iron will has broken her
into a stranger's house.

But it is alright.
By the time she is old she will have woven her soul into a jeweled jacket.
She will have lifted her aura into a bright cap. Her stomach bare,
she will wear America's flag for bottoms, tossing her grin at passing cars
asking for money with a length of cardboard painted red.
"I have awakened!" She will say, "I have opened my eyes!"

Pale Tomatoes, Detergent, New Beer, Cake

I am   drunk   on shopping carts
needing no-one   or not needing at all   a black crow
flies over speaking life   into this terrible
utero

In a place far from   here   a persimmon
floats in wet light   yellow grass in bad ground   makes soil of sun
full seed floating in wind   an early evening
dancer

But sick on street light   ears   buzzing I think
of cicadas   yet the static is thin   a purposeful
lamped electricity   is simulating
the wild

When I enter I'm   zen   could be nothing
if power steering   fluid loneliness didn't   lubricate
my action my go   there was never anything
for me

to do with my hands   so   I pour Coke on
the linoleum   floor as I stare into   the pimpled
face of a bag boy   before waving my
dirty fingers

I am a Jedi   doors   yield and I just leave
wordlessly   fearlessly   into the day
without sun

Late Afternoon in the City

Quails gather beneath young honey-locust trees.
They are a new family with mostly juvenile coats,
though the father has a blue plume
and the mother has a face to match the leaves.

A man who will not see
jogs by with headphones in
causing a stern signal from father bird.

An abrupt migration bleeds out
from the scattered sapling shade and over Latah valley
along the surfaces of broad, straightened cords of sun.

Pissing Near the Tracks of the Union Pacific

On penalty of imprisonment I shalt not trespass
against the rail, but I raise hands
toward this forward lumbering
and breathe my insignificance
inside the sounding pummel of stones
and chokehold of horn.
Two birds fly over, fastened
against the track of gray clouds,
their black feathers extended
above the oil-soaked wood and steel.

A woman in a white blouse
walks through melting snow.
Of course the cars see nothing
and the eyes of the trees
are turned toward heaven,
but she walks. She walks
like money walked the
shadowy sky into this valley,
brought the air alive with
tremors searching out the calm.

Every tribe and tongue and kindred and nation
shall listen to the locomotive
for it has made of them a kingdom.
I had no faith before, but now
this movement overhead, the size of it.
I want to capture your relentless dance,
your forward movement,
all these spliffs of spark,

I want to take them in my mouth!
Reveal a place where I may end
this Adam
who would hide himself from the Train.

Give Thanks

by January's Person

Resting on a rock near a park bench, my cell-phone rings.
I ask the voice on the other end of the line
if it is curious what I am wearing. The voice offers me insurance
for a business I do not own.

We each help others in the ways we can
like this woman, who has just come from her hiding place
in smooth sumac to ask, "Are you alright?"
And how kind of her. Yes, I happen to be.

"Are you alright?" again from the side of her lips.
Yes . . . Yes. I say beautiful day isn't it?
She turns her head, flashing luminous eyes and softly
as to a loved one she clarifies, "Heroin?"

No, I'm sorry. But thank you so much.

Aspen Leaves

As air darkens with storm scent

they shiver. I could say

they sing like the wings

of insects in high brown grass

or flutter like captured moths.

But why should I

say anything? Dusting

my hands.

Where the Soul Might Live

by January's Person

A scissortail hides high in a sycamore—
only now I see three nests just rendered
waiting to be filled. Every tendril in wind creaks
for what will come: the flower, the verdant bud.
I could not waste this life, given like flame
every spring. Sunlight deepens and lightens
the blue, though the moon wanes in my body.
Fungi vibrate in the ground. A bird pecks at snow
evaporating in wind from the south.
My beloved January is sleeping. My beloved
January, where is your soft nothing?
I am afraid. I haven't the will for wakefulness.

Summer in the City

by January's Person

Not really heat I mind but the prodigal, American portion of mid-day when the sun meanders in a cloudless sky as if high on Indica, half asleep believing fully in the rightness of his illumination, his shadow-less truth in the early bird's mouth. I am the worm.

I find the shade of the library sale and pay a dollar to keep Shakespeare out of the incinerator and learn the names of local birds and list various words for reflection. Then, outside, wild-fire smoke seems to bring an early evening. I have come to appreciate living in this valley, which captures so much of the distant forest's pollutant and holds it until rain brings everything to the river. Out here the earth taunts the sun: Single minded man. Mother eater. Infinite child, I burn too. The leaves of just one of my trees can split intentioned light into a bay of luminous creatures.

Invisible Sea

the wind is blowing

            a blue spruce grows on my mind

an itch on my face

but return

the wind is blowing

a red hand blooms from a stem

the wind is blowing

            a building falls out of me

and will disappear

            when I light its old wood on fire

On a Sandbank near the City

I hang my blue tarp from a bent tree
and stare through emptiness in the creek.
Ain't that water so clear, I say to the passing owner of a sad dog.

The human has headphones in. I am invisible
as the highway overhead burns with sound
and trains and planes hide the songs of birds
who could remind me I am not alone.

Somewhere inside, the memory of quietness fills me.
I remember lichened stones, copperheads,
red mud and brown water. Inside me
an old woman is hanging laundry out to dry.

Cold's coming. My hands need
to be knocking on doors. They think
I got four ricks of wood to sell,
running on a stomach half-full of canned meat,

but I'll try to relax now and remember
those wooded hills in Oklahoma
where my travelling ancestors found sleep,
hills who grew me like cane and had no names,
who forgave us our terrible god in the sky
because they just wanted fat, like coyotes in autumn. Though
there weren't no words like autumn.

When that moon came
it was only time to find your gloves
and hope someone loved you enough to knit a hat
or last year left you chain oil or a little cedar to get it started
and oak logs to last the night.

Black Ghosts of Ponderosa on a Silhouette of Hill

—February 29th

by January's Person

No-day now, the dark stones light with green
mosses activating, everything
has been in metamorphosis since January
when time knew me by only the gait of my walk
and called me out of darkness by name.

Even as the sun warms the concrete
the long nights' sensual cold lingers in my clothes.
This city is beautiful in sunlight, but I only want
more of her moments, that passed economy of darkness,
the smoke-filled laughter and blanketed lumen
of eyes in lowlight. January will not fall from my heart.

My shoulders chill against the north-facing moss on a tree.
In the wind I catch the scent of dead wood waking
and the swift river welcoming the birds again.
The sliver of moon is waxing, and I am overcome
with all things returning alive in this light-fall.

Blessed now are the travelers of spirit,
blessed the gathering vagabonds of leaves.
Wild hair and wafting herb are blessed.
All this newness in luminescent grass
feeds on bodies, the bodies of the dead,
and now is just a shadow to speak through.

Gasoline Eyes

When I finished the last strip of grass between the chain-link and highway
I walked by stacked tires and a dumpster smelling like truckers' cigarettes.
Behind large garage doors my father turned a ratchet beneath a semi.
Placing my face on concrete
I saw scuffed shoes and greased hands.
Even then I knew of the woman who was not my mother.

I asked if I could help. His stern voice said, "In a minute."
I'd seen him flare his nostrils and blow out the white dust from the lot
so I did the same. Like my father at break-time, I appreciated
the wall of sticky cassette tapes and breathed the reek of
cheap coffee burning off the maker in the breakroom.
I kicked a crushed coke can across blackened cement until he emerged
and needed me to hold the funnel while he poured gasoline into a jug.

Adamant, I came down on my haunches,
two hands sturdy, intent to keep it steady, but as he poured
I got careless. The liquid weight turned the funnel in my hands
so that it splashed in my face, and my father took his time stopping the flow.

Work that day had made me feel grown,
but my gasoline eyes turned me back
into the wet light of childhood. Sun high and flat white,
I am fearing the loss of a young hickory tree beyond the lot
as my father's stained arms carry me out to the hose.

I Wanted to Teach Her No-one Could Be Lost Who is Remembered

For my daughter
I made mac and cheese with hot dogs in it
and while she ate, reminded her
of her mother.

Remembering to smile, I said, "She gave you your hands"
and chopped broccoli next to the kitchen window
which opened to the stench and cold of the street.
It was getting late. A chill had run from my fingernails
through to the base of my knuckles.

The tenor of birds chirping felt a little like a tenor in rain
and I had to fight the shiver of tears
threatening to erupt from me a little like rain.
That fight still in me and the chorus
of human eyes from the windows of the buildings
and the distant train roaring into the blackened hills were all
a little like rain.

Though the birds quieted down in that steel cloud's arrival
I closed my eyes and listened through the noise
for tenderness in footsteps tapping the brickwork of road.

The birds were ashamed and remained silent
in this passing. The night was crawling into the day.
The sound of cars and blaze of neon lights
would thrive in the coming emptiness of dark.

I wondered if I was old or wise enough yet
to call this city something other than horrible.
A little like rain?
Could I hold my daughter's hand and tell her to be brave
until the train moved on and the birdsongs returned again
like buds on branches in the graying blank of the sky?

Becoming

1.

Like him,
I know the earth and sun can say they love me.

This splintery-tongued son says, I am with you, yes/and…
then stops for fear of cutting.
I want to say I am the mountain
for the same reason he is the sky.

We can't help the world's way. Be sharp, he said so I became
a singing knife. I cannot help but remember
sounding whippoorwills and the sight in childhood
of a fragile little tree frog stuck to light in the window.
I took him on the tip of my blade. Regret

and cicadas were always like silence. Far away
was where the world bloomed.

2. *But Now*

This one, who stood on my father's chest,
I welcome into my tent. Take this bread.
Eat and be full, my fear. I know
you act this way because we thought you were our enemy.

Leather coat, left out in winter rain,
I offer this oil and a dry place.
Flutter in my stomach, disease, what may come,
you may also take my bread, but fear is now my brother.
He will not wake for you.

Welcome rain. Welcome forgotten moon. I have known you.
Welcome night and scaffolding of stars
who shine in reason and without reason.

The heart is this river. The mind is this river.

Grandmother in Fish Lake

Birds give their songs to crickets
as you go blue-black, waist deep,
hand bladed off the forehead.
As you cut caliginous light
I could be the fisherman
on the nearby dock watching you lunge
forward into cold water
your open hands like ladders to a heaven
your arms rounding out from their other.
Yesterday you told me
what you feel near water. Osmosis
a proximity to the dead
in the rapping waves or stillness, the lull and catch.
You said there was something about it all
which made sense.
You hope now I see myself in you, sprawling,
a well-rendered line cut into the
surface of this dark translucent body.
For the witnesses it is this way:
perpetual calling, failing to tire
in the liquid of dusk, a subtlety
as of ancient willows sweeping in the night.

At Home on the Coast (Almost Like Forgetting)

She wants everything to be alright.
And it is.

This place has already mattered.

Remnant of western cedar in pause
Beside the multiform Pacific.

At last the worry goes.

Pale blue sound.

Say I Wandered

from a weak-footed labyrinthian boyhood
up narrow stairs to the smoky air of breakfast
and the voice of my mother
reading her own words.

Say I injured the mouth
of the preacher who had stolen us
and walked with dry bones walking for rain
stumbling out of those doors, unable to hold on.

In every pool and stream, in every lake and river,
I would search for my grandmother who died before I came.
I would try to give her back her scattered children
and the stories. I learned

we were only waves reaching the shore.

How Long It Has Been

Watching cows lay themselves together in grass—
their calmness, like the sun is falling from my shoulders—
it occurs to me; they do not care that it is quiet here
or that terrible sounds shake the earth somewhere else.

They would still conduct themselves this way
say a river had run through the far hillside, or a D9 dozer
had come to take the grass in the neighboring pasture. They would sit
together like this had someone paved over the places they were born.
Because the afternoon is brilliant, and this morning's
chewed cud has afforded rest.

Now the sun is setting, and I am human
and feel the need to crawl further
along the western face of the hill
to capture more of the fleeing
light before it disappears.

How long (how incompletely) have I been imagining this place?
The new dogs whose mother I fed now guard the old logging road.
They are grown with teeth and growling. I pick up a stick.
There are new poisons,
wild green in the streams. My people, their heavenly clarity.

In the valley the beavers have chewed ends of branches,
sharpened, placed. Really nothing has been done.
The pool at the base of Big Round Mountain
has grown a bit broader.

But if I could write what it sounds like—
what it really sounds like—sitting near this dam of sticks
as the creek runs through two days after a storm

I would have no need to call this
the forgotten place or the secret place.
I wouldn't have to say things like, I shall abide
under the shadow of the lichened monoliths. The sky
would be small when I was near mountains
and large when I was not. The sun
peering out from behind clouds
would be better than a vision and less than a gift.

The sound of this creek.
And silence from bare hickory.
From the gully, a gust of wind.

Impermanence

A cat with long hair, calico pattern.
I glance toward setting sun
and turn back to empty sidewalk.

Horsetails Near My New Home

Just over the spent grass
like brooms brushing the edge of the field,
they crescent their tail onto their backs
to shoo flies—
like broken windmills or pulled start string.
They rev with the rhythm of all these birds.
They split through me like the blue jay caw.

In the high trunk of a dead oak tree
sun on a bat house is dreaming.
A pause, a ripple, ancient
water spilling up as dew.
The autumn comes down now. Down here this means
a slight respite of flower before the dead train arrives
from the west, the marigolds still yellow
before the various ice houses the branches.

But still now. Still
we've earned this day, just not sweltering,
by bearing August's dry, baking fields.
Bitter joy, the caterpillars have come back to the brassicas
and the tomatoes have started popping off again.

Here in the slow heart of half heat
I might say I have wasted my life.
I might say this with an animal tongue, say it smiling.
That ol' boy, my life, who sleeps in the sun,
caste of the earth, that product of my parents' empty work
who cannot rest nor waste,
or, as harvest itself, hasn't time enough to know.

Persimmons

Just before the leaves fall,
after countless hours in sugar-filling zeniths,
the black/green caps of petals curl.

Our trees have carried their fruits beyond bitterness.
These luminaries under gentle folds of ash
foretell the harvest moon.

We toss stones, or leap, fingers outstretched.
We shake the branches,
and the little ones hold out their hands.

These same bright children of the woods
who puckered impatient mouths through August
now sweetened rest. Without sadness,
                                        they will soon let go entirely.

Ceremony

A boy uses a stick
to dig a narrow hole
in the loam beneath cedars
breaking the thread-like white of mycelium
which reactivates
around the body of a squirrel
he found dead on the road
far from home
in the hush of rain.

Acknowledgments

The author would like to thank the publications in which some of these poems first appeared, sometimes in different versions.

Abandon Journal: "Snow Falls from Branches," "Black Ghosts of Ponderosa on a Silhouette of Hill"

About Place Journal: "Grandmother in Fish Lake"

Cimarron Review: "Migrating Psalm"

Hawaii Pacific Review: "At the Confluence of Latah Creek and the Spokane"

Heron Tree: "What She Said When I First Came to the Community"

Indiana Voice Journal: "He Knew No Haste"

Mid/South Sonnets: A Belle Point Press Anthology: "Mush"

The Pacific Northwest Inlander: "Where the Soul Might Live"

The Swamp: "The Dirt Road as Threshold"

Thrush: "Ceremony"

DAMIEN URIAH is a poet, teacher, regenerative farmer, and musician. Their work can be found in *Cimarron Review*, *Hawaii Pacific Review*, *Thrush*, *Heron Tree*, *About Place Journal*, and many other publications. Damien grew up on the Cherokee Nation side of the Ozark mountains and has lived, written, and worked in various places, including in their second land-love, the Pacific Northwest. Currently a professor of writing at the University of Arkansas-Fort Smith, Damien lives with his wife and many plants and animals on a small eco-farm near his childhood home in northeastern Oklahoma.

Belle Point Press is a literary small press along the Arkansas-Oklahoma border. Our mission is simple: Stick around and read. Learn more at bellepointpress.com.